Class 40 Country
WALES

Contents

1. Introduction   *3*
2. North Wales   *4*
3. Cambrian coast & Central Wales   *75*
4. South & West Wales   *82*

Published by

Ty Mawr Publications
Holmes Chapel
Cheshire
UK
www.tymawrpublications.co.uk
© 2015 Steve Morris

ISBN
978-0-9552354-8-1

Design & typesetting by
Steve Morris

Printed by Cambrian Printers
Aberystwyth

ALL RIGHTS RESERVED

No part of this publication may be reproduced, stored in a retrieval system, or transmitted, in any form or by any means, electronic, mechanical, photocopying, recording or otherwise, without prior permission in writing from the publisher.

Above. 40162 climbs out of Holyhead working 1J53, the 16.30 to Manchester Victoria. August 22nd 1982. **Steve Morris.**

Front cover.
40024 "Lucania" is well off the beaten track as it approaches Swansea heading "The South Wales Whistler" tour on April 28th 1984. Originating in Leeds, 40024 would work back from the final destination of Carmarthen having run light from Swansea following 37267 which had worked the tour into West Wales. **Steve Morris.**

Back cover.
Saturday November 30th 2002 was a milestone in the history of the CFPS with the return of 40145 to mainline passenger duty by working The Christmas Cracker 1V railtour. Starting at Crewe it ran via Birmingham to Holyhead with the return via Manchester Victoria and Birmingham. In this view 40145 is seen on the outbound working back where it belongs on the approach to Penmaenmawr. **Martin Loader.**

Acknowledgements
This publication would not have been possible without the support of many. It has given people that have not had their material published in the past the opportunity to showcase some of their collection, many thanks to you and my more regular contributors for your assistance, it is as ever, much appreciated. Apologies to those who submitted material that was not used, space constraints are to blame but rest assured everything is being kept on file for future projects!
Other than raising funds for the CFPS the main aim of this project was to produce something with input from those with a particular affection for Class 40's, for the benefit of all that fit into that category. Having used material from more than forty different sources I think this aim has been achieved! I hope the facts contained within are accurate but as ever please feel free to drop me a line via the Ty Mawr Publications website with any corrections or otherwise!

Steve Morris, Holmes Chapel, February 2015.
www.tymawrpublications.co.uk

References
The allocation history of BR Diesels & Electrics by Roger Harris. Class 40 Motherlist by Alan Wilson, www.class40motherlist.com

INTRODUCTION

Welcome to the first book produced by Ty Mawr Publications on behalf of The Class Forty Preservation Society (CFPS). The aim of this project is to raise funds for the continued upkeep of CFPS owned 40135 and 40145 with 100% of the sales income being used for this purpose. This is the 4th book to be produced by the CFPS and follows on from the three previous ones released a few years ago to celebrate 50 years of class 40 operation. It is hoped to release up to four volumes as and when material becomes available. The success of this venture depends on the supply of images covering Class 40 operation throughout the country so if you have anything that you think would be of interest please contact me via the Ty Mawr Publications website or the CFPS. The first of this series covers an area that in many parts was a stronghold for the class throughout their period of regular use from the early 1960's through to the mid 1980's, Wales! Other areas I hope to cover are Scotland, the London Midland and Eastern Regions. This will provide an opportunity for the modern traction enthusiast to put together a comprehensive record of the routine and more unusual workings covered by this popular class of locomotive throughout the country.

Above. Early days! September 1959 and brand new Carlisle Upperby based D230 (40030), later named "Scythia", has just arrived at Llandudno Junction for gauging trials west of the area. Here it can be seen outside Llandudno Junction shed with a number of Holyhead footplate staff in attendance. This includes, 4th from left, Driver Will "Bach" Jones who had driven D230 over to North Wales and Instructor David Manley Williams in the cab.
The initial batch of drivers in Wales to be trained on class 40's were based at Holyhead and Llandudno Junction. In October 1959 D233 (40033), later "Empress of England" was based at Holyhead for this purpose.
On May 6th 1960 D230 would be the first of the class to visit St Pancras station by working the 11.42 from Manchester Victoria throughout. Withdrawal would come after 23 years service in April 1983.
Garnedd Jones collection.

North Wales

North Wales was the part of The Principality most associated with Class 40's, having taken over Irish Mail and Emerald Isle Express passenger workings between Holyhead and Euston on April 25th 1960. Possibly the first passenger working took place on August 8th 1959 when D222 (40022) worked the 1.20pm Crewe to Llandudno service. The use of the class along the North Wales Coast route expanded throughout the 1960's and into the 70's during which time they were responsible for a wide range of workings from top link passenger duties through to various freight services including cattle trains and Freightliner workings in and out of Holyhead port. Confirmation of the popularity of the class in the area can be seen at the time of the Britannia bridge fire on May 23rd 1970 when seven of them were marooned on Anglesey as a result of the bridge closure, namely 219/231/232/233/241/307 and 390. They were all returned to the mainland via boat from Holyhead to Barrow during June of that year. In addition to regular workings across the North Wales Coast, Class 40's were also used throughout their career on a variety of freight duties in and out of Dee Marsh and on the lines around Wrexham into the likes of Croes Newydd yard, Brymbo steelworks and Bersham colliery.

Passenger workings continued right up to the end of their regular use in January 1985. The final working out of Holyhead prior to withdrawal of the class in January 1985 was 40086 heading the 1G00 01.25 relief to Birmingham as far as Crewe on January 4th of that year. However, the final timetabled passenger working of all in North Wales fell to 40152 which headed 1E93 the 17.30 Bangor to York on January 17th following the failure of the booked class 47. The last recorded freight working out of Holyhead involved 40060 with a special Freightliner to York Holgate sidings on January 6th 1985 whilst the final North Wales working of all (D200, 40145 and the four departmental 40's apart) occurred on Monday January 21st when 40143 worked west on the 1D00 "Bangor papers" from Manchester Victoria before returning to Crewe on the 3A19 empty stock and being withdrawn from service the following day.

Below. Holyhead shed fuelling point, March 16th 1977. 40004 and 40012 "Aureol" are being serviced prior to taking up their next duties. Both examples were regular visitors to North Wales throughout their life with 40012 even making it to Valley as late as July 25th 1985. This was whilst in departmental use as 97407 together with 97406 (40060) on a train of track panels. **Steve Morris.**

North Wales

Above. Having worked into North Wales on the weekly petroleum coke to Anglesey Aluminium, Healey Mills based 40002 sits outside Holyhead shed. Originating in Immingham it would have taken over this working from a Class 76 at Godley Junction. The date is May 29th 1978 and apart from appearances on this working, Eastern Region Class 40's were rare visitors to Holyhead whilst visits to Llandudno on summer Saturday passenger duties were more common. **Steve Morris.**

Below. Longsight based example 222 (40022) "Laconia" is stabled outside Holyhead shed during the summer of 1973. The nameplate has recently been removed from this side although the one on the other (B bank) side would remain in place until the end of 1974. **Pat Webb.**

North Wales

Above. A very early image of D220 (40020) on Holyhead shed during a period when steam still reigned supreme. The date is August 1960 only four months after the class took over key passenger duties between Holyhead and London Euston. D220 would be named "Franconia" in February 1963 and remain in traffic until withdrawal on August 27th 1982. **Peter Sedge.**

Below. North Wales Coast favourite 40033 "Empress of England" stabled inside Holyhead shed alongside 47468 on December 16th 1983. See also page 12 and 18. **Steve Morris.**

North Wales

Above. August 1st 1987 and 40122 waits departure from Holyhead on 1A56 the 12.45 for Euston with Drivers John Jones and Bill Doutch in view. This would be the last time a 40 would head a Euston service out of Holyhead without another loco in the consist, 40122 repeating it one more time the following February with 47427 in tow. **Garnedd Jones.**

Below. 40069 approaches Holyhead station on the 2D69 12.40 departure from Llandudno Junction on June 27th 1982. Note the bedplate oil drain pipe modification running beneath the solebar, thankfully a one off, although it did make identification of this loco very easy! **Peter Hanahoe.**

North Wales

Above. 331 (40131) waits departure from Holyhead platform 2 with an afternoon boat train for Euston during July 1972. **Will Welch.**

Below. June 26th 1980. 40145 departs Holyhead on the Ford company container train with its distinctive green containers. Within four years it would become CFPS property! **Colin Webb.**

North Wales

Above. The final double headed Class 40 service to depart Holyhead. Here 40196 and 40080 can be seen leaving the town on 1A56, the 13.10 Euston service on July 30th 1983. It is 18 months before the end of regular Class 40 operation but passenger duties for the class in and out of Holyhead were already getting rarer so this working was particularly notable.

Below. 40097 ended its career at Holyhead, having derailed on the approach to the town whilst working the down Trafford Park Freightliner during the evening of May 16th 1983. It was stored at Holyhead for several days before being withdrawn at the end of June. In this view the re railing process is progressing the day after the incident. **Both Pat Webb.**

North Wales

Above. 40172 on the outskirts of Holyhead heading the 12.55 departure for Crewe on August 8th 1982. Derailment damage would end its career just over 12 months later with cutting up coming soon after at Doncaster Works in February 1984.

Below. Having been held alongside Ty Mawr Farm, the 10.45 Manchester Victoria to Holyhead starts its final approach to Holyhead behind 40194 on July 24th 1982. **Both Steve Morris.**

North Wales

Above. Haymarket based 40168 is well off the beaten track as it departs Holyhead on a Trafford Park bound Freightliner on March 5th 1978. A Scottish Region locomotive since introduction at the end of 1961, it would move south to Longsight in October 1981 and remain in service there until November 1984, a few weeks before the end of regular Class 40 operation. The end came in The Melts at Crewe Works during August 1986. **Steve Morris.**

Below. Following the end of the class 24's and demotion of the class 40's to more freight duties they became regular performers on nuclear flask traffic out of Valley sidings. In this view a flask recently delivered by road from Wylfa power station is seen being loaded onto a Sellafield bound flask wagon headed by 40129. The date is June 1982 and some years before the start of block trains conveying this cargo commenced. **Barry Wynne.**

North Wales

Above. June 13th 1970 and 233 (40033) "Empress of England" is in the process of having its bogies removed in Valley sidings to allow it to be shipped to Barrow following the Britannia Bridge fire of May 23rd. It was one of seven of the class to be so affected, the others being 219/231/232/241/307 and 390. **Ron Watson-Jones.**

Right. 40145 powers through Valley working "The Pennine Fellsman" tour to Durham on May 25th 2009. With load 12 plus 47815 on the back this was a real test, but no problem! **Garnedd Jones.**

Below. 40184 passes RAF Valley heading 1J50, the 14.44 Holyhead to Manchester Victoria on August 22nd 1984. Withdrawal from service would come less than four months later. **Steve Morris.**

North Wales

Above. An early 1960's view of D223 (40023) "Lancastria" heading an up Irish Mail through Ty Croes on Anglesey. By now Class 40's were responsible for working the vast majority of Holyhead to Euston services although it would be several years before steam traction would disappear completely, the final working not taking place until early August 1967. **Barry Wynne.**

Below. Ty Croes again but some twenty years later on July 13th 1983. The CFPS's very own 40135 is seen heading for Holyhead on the 4D59 Freightliner working from Trafford Park. Class 40's were regular performers on these duties throughout their career. **Peter Hanahoe.**

North Wales

Above. D295 (40095) exits Bodorgan Tunnel on a stopping service during 1963. 40095 would be a relatively early withdrawal, coming in September 1981 as life expired at Wigan Springs Branch.

Below. D219 (40019) "Caronia" working a relief to The Irish Mail is seen about to start climbing Llangaffo bank during the summer of 1963. Evidence of a recent Royal Train duty can be seen. **Both Barry Wynne.**

North Wales

Above. "The Amlwch Pioneer" originating at Euston was the first Diesel hauled passenger train to traverse the Amlwch Branch, one of several Class 40 hauled railtours to do so during the 1980's. Here it can be seen behind 40058 approaching Gaerwen Junction at start of the branch with 40034 in the loop ready to be attached to the rear of the train for the journey to Amlwch. May 14th 1983. **Peter Hanahoe.**

Below. The second tour to visit Amlwch was run on July 3rd 1983 as "The Menai Marauder". Starting from Plymouth it was top and tailed along the Amlwch branch by 40028 and 40093. In this view it can be seen heading for Amlwch with 40093 on the tail. **Colin Webb.**

North Wales

Above. July 24th 1984. 40181 drifts down into the Cefni Valley at Pentre Berw Llanerchymedd with 7D04, the morning Llandudno Junction to Amlwch goods. Originating at Ellesmere Port it is hauling empty grey tanks for carrying ethylene dibromide from Associated Octel Amlwch, and white tanks full of liquid chlorine to the plant. A pool of 39 two axle air braked TTA tanks were used in this traffic from the 1970's onwards, 20 and 19 for the ethylene dibromide and chlorine traffic respectively. A brake van was attached at each end of the train to facilitate a reversal at Hooton and barrier wagons were included due the hazardous nature of the cargo. **Peter Hanahoe.**

Below. A rare view of a working into the siding off the Amlwch branch at Rhosgoch during the construction of a tank farm. This was to store crude oil which had been pumped ashore at Amlwch, before being piped to the Shell Stanlow refinery. Several trains associated with the laying of the pipeline to Stanlow ran from Rhydymwyn near Mold during the mid 1970's (see page 70). In this view, 40113 is seen removing empty wagons from the siding prior to propelling the loaded ones back in. The development of Supertankers that could not moor off Amlwch spelt the end of this facility before it really got going and the site was only used for a short period before being closed down. **E N Kneale/Steve Morris collection.**

North Wales

Left. A significant Class 40 working took place on July 1st 1969 when 233 (40033) "Empress of England" and 216 (40016) "Campania" worked the Prince of Wales' Investiture train from Euston to Caernarvon. Here they can be seen arriving at a temporary platform built at Griffiths Crossing just outside the town to allow the Royal Family to disembark ready for the short tip to the Castle.
Steve Morris collection.

Above. D212 (40012) "Aureol" races through Menai Bridge station on a down working for Holyhead during the early 1960's.

Below. An afternoon Holyhead to Euston boat train is seen running through the centre road at Bangor in the summer of 1963 with D319 (40119) in charge. It would work right through to the capital with the Holyhead or Camden crew.
Both E N Kneale/Steve Morris collection.

North Wales

Above. D297 (40097) calls at Bangor on a Holyhead to Manchester working during 1963. This particular example would end its useful life following a derailment in Holyhead twenty years later, see page 9. **Barry Wynne.**

Below. An unidentified "namer" prepares to move the stock for a Bangor to Manchester service over to platform 1 during a winters evening in 1980. Class 40's were diagrammed for these duties through to 30th May 1981 when 40004 headed the last booked Class 40 working, the 1D21, 15.40 from Manchester Victoria and 1J31 1925 return. Appearances would however continue for several more years covering for non available booked motive power. **E N Kneale/Steve Morris collection.**

North Wales

Above. April 29th 1983. 40063 is on the approach to Menai Bridge working 4D58, the 14.40 Freightliner service from Birmingham Lawley Street to Holyhead. A steadfast Haymarket based locomotive for over 20 years, transfer south to Wigan took place in October 1981 and within twelve months of this image being recorded withdrawal came from Longsight.

Below. The final Vacuum Only braked member of the class was 40009, remaining in service until as late as November 7th 1984. In this view it can be seen in Bangor with the 1J09 empty newspaper vans for Manchester Red Bank on July 20th 1983. **Both Peter Hanahoe.**

North Wales

Above. May 16th 1970. A classic study of 216 (40016) "Campania" waiting to depart Bangor on a an up parcels duty. A week later Bangor became the terminus for North Wales Coast workings due to the Britannia Bridge fire which severed the rail link to Anglesey for over 18 months. The loco still shows signs of a Royal Train duty. This was during a period when "Campania" was one of a small number in the pool of Class 40's used for such workings. See also page 18.

Below. A superb view of an unidentified 40 which has just exited Bangor Tunnel heading through Maesgerchen on the outskirts of the town with a Manchester bound service. Summer of 1980. **Both Barry Wynne.**

North Wales

Above. 40025 "Lusitania" powers through Glan-y-Môr Elias on the approach to Bangor working the 1D21 1540 from Manchester Victoria. The date is April 27th 1981, just a few more weeks of regular class 40 haulage on these duties remain.

Below. 26th October 1983 and 40126 heads the morning Holyhead to Llandudno Junction 7T30 trip working past what was Penrhyn sidings near Bangor. Amongst the consist can be seen cement empties from Bangor, fuel empties from Holyhead shed and loaded Cargowagons from Anglesey Aluminium near Holyhead. **Both Peter Hanahoe.**

North Wales

Above. The last double headed Class 40 working in North Wales took place on July 25th 1985 when departmental examples 97407(40012) and 97405 (40060) worked a train of track panels in tandem from Crewe to Valley. Here they can be seen later that day at Talybont near Bangor running light back to Crewe as 0X41 from Valley with Driver Mike Lunn up front and Kevin Aitcheson following with second man Gareth Parry.

Below. 40172 passes Wîg Crossing Llanfairfechan with the Associated Octel Amlwch to Llandudno Junction sulphur empties on 15th July 1983. These wagons would eventually end up at Mostyn Docks for loading and return to Amlwch a few days later. **Both Peter Hanahoe.**

North Wales

Above. Early evening on May 24th 1983, Pentre Du crossing Llanfairfechan. 40050 applies the power heading the 15.54 4D59 Manchester Trafford Park to Holyhead service. Ten weeks service remained for 40050 before withdrawal from duty at Longsight depot. **Peter Hanahoe.**

Below. A rare view of Haymarket stalwart 40165 in North Wales. The date is August 28th 1979 and it has found itself on the 15.40 Manchester to Bangor, seen skirting the coast on Pen-y-Clip viaduct near Llanfairfechan. This was an exceptionally rare working for this loco and was followed by the 19.30 return. 40165 was back in North Wales on the 30th turning up on the 17.18 Llandudno to Manchester before being sent home via a parcels working to Cumbria. **Ron Watson-Jones.**

North Wales

Above. June 13th 1964 and D211 (40011) "Mauretania" heads through Penmaenmawr on a down evening stopping service. An early candidate for withdrawal, 40011 ended its days as a Healey Mills based loco on October 5th 1980 with less than 20 years service under its belt! **Peter Owen.**

Below. 40019 "Caronia" is seen assisting an ailing Park Royal DMU at Penmaenmawr during the summer of 1981. Within a few months this example would be withdrawn, cutting taking place at Doncaster Works in February 1984. **Ron Watson-Jones.**

North Wales

Above. Departmental operated 97408 (40118) is seen with its train being loaded with ballast, final destination Crewe Gresty Green, on July 30th 1985. It was not as frequent a visitor to North Wales as the other three examples of this sub class namely 97405 (40060), 97406 (40135) and 97407 (40012). 40118 remains intact undergoing restoration at Tyseley. **Ron Watson-Jones.**

Below. D337 (40137) has just passed through Penmaenmawr on the "Horse and Carriage" from Holyhead. This was the midday ECS/parcels departure that ran to Manchester Ordsall Lane picking up as it went along, often resulting in a lengthy consist by the time it reached its destination. Date, 18th April 1964. **Peter Owen.**

North Wales

North Wales

Above. A prime example of what was possible in "the good old days"! To celebrate 25 years of Class 40 operation, local resident and Class 40 enthusiast Ron Watson-Jones created a headboard to mark the occasion and fitted it to 40082 working a Penmaenmawr to St Helens ballast on May the 5th 1983. Rather than let it go all the way to its destination it was removed after a short distance for safe keeping. In this view the train is seen having pulled up on the approach to Penmaenbach tunnel at Dwygyfylchi with the ever obliging traincrew about to return the headboard to its creator! As some readers will know, Ron was also responsible for stencilling the names on previously named 40's, most of which were applied in Penmaenmawr yard whilst on various ballast workings.

Page 28 top. November 12th 1987 was a busy day for 40122. It started with a light engine move from Birmingham New Street to Bescot having just worked in on an overnight parcels train from Reading. This was followed by a Speedlink working to Basford Hall before heading to Gresty Green to collect ballast empties for onward working to Penmaenmawr. In this view it can be seen later that day in Penmaenmawr yard being loaded ready for the 7K11 back to Crewe Gresty Green. Crewe Diesel depot then carried out a B exam on 122 before it headed back to Penmaenmawr on the same working the next day.

Page 28 bottom. April 23rd 1981 near Dwygyfylchi. 40177 heads for Llandudno Junction heading the afternoon Associated Octel Amlwch to Llandudno Junction service conveying loaded ethylene dibromide tanks (grey colour) and empty liquid chlorine tanks (white). Final destination would be Ellesmere Port. The last such working ran on February 10th 1994 with transfer of the business to the much "safer" and more "environmentally friendly" road transport! By 2003 the Octel plant had disappeared so ending 130 years of operation for the Amlwch Branch. **All Ron Watson-Jones.**

North Wales

Above. 40101 pauses at Penmaenmawr on 1J30, the 11.30 Bangor to Manchester working on April 26th 1980. It would also cover the afternoon return Manchester to Bangor working as well. Haymarket based at the time this would have been an unusual turn for it to appear on but this was as a result of being in the area following attention at Crewe Works.

Below. 40063 is seen heading for St Helens on a ballast train from Penmaenmawr about to enter Penmaenbach Tunnel on July 27th 1983. At the time this was one of several such Class 40 hauled turns in and out of Penmaenmawr yard resulting in up to three examples per day arriving at the quarry loading site. **Both Ron Watson-Jones.**

North Wales

Above. July 22nd 1963 near Conwy. D269 (40069) heads the up "Welshman" to Euston. Conveying portions from Holyhead, Pwllheli, Porthmadog, and Llandudno this service ended the following year after closure of the line from Caernarvon to Afonwen. **Peter Owen.**

Below. D334 (40134) passes Conwy castle heading for Holyhead during the early 1960's. The last coach has just exited Robert Stephenson's tubular bridge. Opened in 1849 this remains a familiar landmark on the North Wales Coast route. **Ken Wood collection.**

North Wales

Above. Llandudno Junction 28th March 1981. 40057 approaches the station on an extra "Liner" from Holyhead. The following year, along with 40084, it would gain celebrity status as one of a pair of Gateshead based 40's specially prepared for railtour duties. **Peter Hanahoe.**

Below. D214 (40014) "Antonia" is paired up with Haymarket allocated 368 (40168) which is on test following classified repair at Crewe Works during March 1971. The service was the 14.57 Bangor to Euston which along with the inbound 09.35 from Euston was regularly used for this purpose from and to Crewe at the time. **Ron Watson-Jones.**

North Wales

Above. During the summer of 1985 40122 was diagrammed for several Stoke-on-Trent to Llandudno return and fill in Llandudno to Blaenau Ffestiniog turns. The final one that year took place on the 12th of September. During the day it was used to work a failed DMU to Llandudno Junction, seen here, after working 2D18 the 13.30 Blaenau Ffestiniog to Llandudno. That night 40122 worked the 6V86 Basford Hall to Severn Tunnel Junction although this was assisted by 47254 from Hereford due to lack of crew knowledge. The journey home took it via Old Oak Common and Willesden before taking up duties on the Leeds to Carlisle circuit!

Below. January 15th 1985. A week of regular Class 40 action remains when 40060 prepares to depart Llandudno Junction on the daily Speedlink service to Warrington Arpley. Within a few months it would be back in the area as departmental operated 97405 with regular duties in and out of Penmaenmawr quarry loading point a feature. **Both Ron Watson-Jones.**

North Wales

Above. 40035 "Apapa" heads the Ffestiniog Pullman charter to Blaenau Ffestiniog through Roman Bridge station on June 6th 1982. Starting at Euston, 40106 was also used on this service between Crewe and Llandudno Junction. **Ron Fisher.**

Below left. Heading for Blaenau Ffestiniog, CFPS owned 40145 passes Glan Conwy working "The Whistling Slater" charter on June 4th 2005. Holyhead was also visited during the day. **Phil Wright.**

Below right. Prior to the withdrawal of D200/40122, several farewell railtours were organised. Quite rightly one of these reached Holyhead, running as "The Tubular Belle" tour on April 2nd 1988. It also visited Llandudno and Blaenau Ffestiniog during the day. Here it can be seen in typical Conwy Valley weather at Dolwyddelan. **Peter Hanahoe.**

North Wales

Above. From May 1982, "Trip 47" from Llandudno Junction was booked for a Class 40. Amongst other things this involved running to Trawsfynydd to pick up flasks from the local nuclear power station. In this view taken during 1982, 40126 nears Blaenau Ffestiniog en route from Trawsfynydd conveying a single flask to Llandudno Junction. Final destination was Sellafield for reprocessing.

Below. 40030 is seen engaged in changes to the site of Blaenau Ffestiniog station during 1981. In 1982 this resulted in the opening of a new station on the site of the old GWR "Central" station and an interchange with the Ffestiniog narrow gauge railway. **Both Merfyn Jones.**

North Wales

Above. Kicking off from Bristol Temple Meads at 05.36, 40145 is seen later in the day approaching Dolwyddelan on the return from Blaenau Ffestiniog with Pathfinder Tours' 1Z52 13:26 Blaenau Ffestiniog to Holyhead 'Whistling Slater' railtour. June the 4th 2005. See also p34. **Martin Loader.**

Below. During two weekends in October 1983, bogie rotational tests were carried out on 56042 between Roman Bridge and Betws-y-Coed as part of work on what would eventually become the class 58 CP3 bogie. On the weekend of October 30th, 40004 was chosen to assist with the project and in this view it is seen at Roman Bridge during the work. **Peter Hanahoe.**

North Wales

Above. June 16th 1973. 314 (40114) has derailed on the approach to Llandudno station whilst working the 10.40 from Manchester Victoria. Passengers were detrained and led on foot to the station platform without any drama. Imagine that happening today! **The late Keith Holt.**

Below. Ex works 40115 waits departure from Llandudno on the 17.40 for Stoke on August 29th 1979. A London Midland loco throughout its career, withdrawal came from Longsight depot in March 1982 although it would be a further six years before disposal at Crewe Works. **Alan Lea.**

North Wales

North Wales

Above. D343 (40143) heads an up Irish Mail out of Llandudno Junction on July 26th 1963. Later in life it would work the last Class 40 hauled train in North Wales during regular service for the class. This was from Bangor on the 3A19 "empty papers" to Crewe late on January 21st 1985, Before immediate withdrawal. **Peter Owen.**

Left. May 23rd 1980 and 40141 prepares to leave Llandudno in multiple with 40024 on the 18.17 for Manchester Victoria. Earlier that day they had worked in from Crewe and Manchester Victoria respectively before being teamed up to return east. **Arnie Furness.**

Below. Having worked in from Bradford earlier in the day, see page 52, D397 (40197) of Healey Mills is seen leaving Llandudno Junction on the 10th of July 1971 returning east on the 1E82 13.25 Llandudno to Newcastle service. **The late Keith Holt.**

North Wales

Above. Having visited Blaenau Ffestiniog, "The Tubular Belle" railtour of April 2nd 1988, see also page 34, is seen on the approach to Llandudno Junction en route Holyhead before a return to Crewe to hand over to 85006 for the final leg to Euston. **Garnedd Jones.**

Below. 40055 approaches Llandudno Junction on 4D59, the afternoon Freightliner working from Manchester Trafford Park to Holyhead on 14th February 1981. **Peter Hanahoe.**

North Wales

Above. D292 (40092) is seen between Colwyn Bay and Llandudno Junction at Mochdre working a down express on July 20th 1963. This part of the route was re aligned in 1984 as part of the A55 road upgrade work. Withdrawn from service on 28th November 1982 it was subsequently used during re-railing exercises at Temple Mills yard in March 1984 before a move to Swindon Works via Reading depot for disposal, something that was completed by the middle of March 1986.

Below. May 18th 1964. D297 (40097) is on the final approach to Llandudno Junction heading a down relief express for Holyhead. **Both Peter Owen.**

North Wales

Above. 12th June 1982, Colwyn Bay. 40020 "Franconia" heads for Bangor with a working from Manchester Victoria. Withdrawn from Longsight just over two years later it would then languish in Crewe Works for a further five years before being cut up.

Below. 40143 on the outskirts of Colwyn Bay with 1M59, the 09.08 Scarborough to Llandudno working on July 11th 1981. **Both Peter Hanahoe.**

North Wales

Above. 40183 at Old Colwyn on the approach to Penmaenrhos tunnel working 1Z34, a charter taking cruise ship passengers from Holyhead to Edinburgh. Note the bogie van behind the loco for carrying the luggage. It is July 3rd 1982 and works associated with the new A55 Expressway are well underway. **Peter Hanahoe.**

Below. Llandulas, July 28th 1979. Healey Mills based 40114 climbs up towards Penmaenrhos tunnel working the 11.05 Manchester Victoria to Holyhead. An early candidate for withdrawal, the end came in October 1980 following less than twenty years active service. **David Rostance.**

North Wales

Above. Having just exited Penmaenrhos tunnel, 40155 is seen passing Llysfaen signal box working the 11.30 Bangor to Manchester. Llysfaen station closed in 1931 but the signal box, originally built to service the long closed ICI limestone works opposite, stayed in use until 1983. July 7th 1979.

Below. July 28th 1979 and Springs Branch based 40185 has just passed Abergele on a Holyhead bound Freightliner working. Opened in the late 1960's, the container terminal at Holyhead closed on March 18th 1991, the final working departing at 19.15 behind Tinsley's 47301. This was to allow development of the land to accommodate the new HSS dock facilities. **Both David Rostance.**

North Wales

Above. A classic mid 60's view taken on July 23rd 1966 of D226 (40026) passing Abergele at the head of a lengthy up ECS working comprising of about 20 coaches! Originally destined to be named "Media" this never materialised although the plates were cast. Following a period in store during 1976, 40026 was reinstated and ran for a further four years before withdrawal in April 1980.

Below. Saturday July 11th 1970. A unidentified 40 heads west through Abergele with rake of rail blue and maroon MK1's in tow, probably full of day trippers for Llancudno.
Both the late Keith Holt.

North Wales

Above. 40023 "Lancastria" leaves a smokescreen over Rhyl as it heads west with a Manchester to Holyhead service on August 3rd 1974.

Below. On the same day, Healey Mills based 40102 is seen at the same location heading a summer Saturday service to Llandudno. In 1976, collision damaged locos apart, 40102 was one of nine 40's withdrawn from service as surplus to requirements, the others being 40005/021/039/041/043/045/053 and 089. 40102 had only given just over 15 years service! **Both Steve Morris collection.**

North Wales

Above. The summer of 1966 and another view of D223 (40023) "Lancastria" at Rhyl, this time making an evening departure on a special working. Corporate blue and grey is just starting to appear on the stock behind. See also page 14. **Steve Morris collection**.

Below. 40046 heads the 11.11 Manchester Victoria to Holyhead out of Rhyl on June 24th 1978. Healey Mills based at the time this would have been a relatively rare passenger working for the loco west of Llandudno Junction. Interestingly, following withdrawal on February 20th 1983 it was put into departmental use as a training locomotive at the S.A.S Headquarters in Moreton-on-Lugg for three years. Final cutting came at Vic Berry's Leicester at the end of 1987. **David Rostance.**

North Wales

Above. August Bank Holiday 1966 and a pair of "Whistlers" speed through the centre road at Rhyl on a relief to the Irish Mail from Holyhead. The leading loco seems to have recently received works attention and could possibly have been on test. **Dave Marks.**

Below. 201 (40001) calls at Rhyl with the 09.44 Holyhead to Euston on Saturday June 16th 1973. Withdrawn from service at the end of July 1984 it was then dumped at Carlisle Kingmoor and used as a source of spares for sister loco D200 for several years. **The late Keith Holt.**

North Wales

Above. 40057 sits in the up through line at Rhyl whilst engaged in Pway duties during the spring of 1984. A few months later bogie fractures would end its career, a curse that resulted in the end for many class 40's over the years. 40057 had travelled to many parts in West Wales during September of the previous year, see page 96. **Don Gatehouse.**

Below. June 16th 1973. 234 (40034) "Accra" prepares to call at Rhyl whilst working the 08.28 Birmingham to Llandudno service. The "A bank" side nameplate would remain fitted until early 1974 whilst the other side had already been "liberated" by March 1970! **The late Keith Holt.**

North Wales

Above. 40010 "Empress of Britain" heads out of Rhyl on the 09.37 Llandudno to Birmingham New Street. A cracked main generator spelt the end for it as early as July 1981. **David Rostance.**

Below. 28th August 1982 and celebrity 40106 is seen at Prestatyn working 1J30, the 11.57 Bangor to Manchester Victoria. Two return trips were covered by 106 that particular day with a return to Holyhead on the following one. Apart from accident victim D322, 40106 was one of two Class 40's never to carry BR blue livery, the other being early withdrawal candidate 40039. **Peter Hanahoe.**

North Wales

Above. North Wales regular 40033 "Empress of England" heads out of Prestatyn on 1J31 the 19.25 Bangor to Manchester during the summer of 1981. **The late Joe House**.

Below. All is clearly not well with 40015 "Aquitania" whilst working 1J22, the 13.49 Bangor to Manchester Victoria. A complete failure was the verdict! 40091 was then provided to remove the errant loco before normal service was resumed behind 40002. April 7th 1983. **Gary Spain.**

North Wales

The images on the next two pages were all taken by the late **Keith Holt** during a summer Saturday at Prestatyn on **July 10th 1971**. They act as a reminder of days gone by when numerous Class 40 hauled passenger services could be seen in North Wales. A number of the locos concerned would be from Eastern region depots such as York and Healey Mills having a day out to transport many Yorkshire holiday makers to resorts across the coast to Llandudno with other services heading to Holyhead for onward transit to Ireland.

Above. A fine study of D397 (40197) slowing to a stop at Prestatyn working the 1M90 Bradford to Llandudno. Right through to the early 1980's, summer Saturdays in North Wales provided an ideal opportunity to witness Eastern Region class 40's, many normally used on freight duties, in action. See page 39 for the return working.

North Wales

Above. D328 (40128) departs Prestatyn on the 1G10 from Llandudno heading for Birmingham.

Page 52 bottom. Before ending its life in Scotland, D373 (40173) was a Longsight loco at the time of this working. Here it is seen at Prestatyn on the 1A35 09.15 Bangor to Euston service. Withdrawn in August 1981 it languished at Eastfield for several years during which time it acted amongst other things as a convenient place for the author to grab forty winks on nights during tea break whilst working there in the summer of 1982!

Below. Our last look at a typical 1970's summer Saturday at Prestatyn and a particularly shabby D334 (40134) leaves the town working 1K06 an additional service from Llandudno to Stoke. Unofficially named "Andromeda" later in life it would have a relatively short career of just over twenty years before withdrawal from Longsight.

North Wales

Above. The final Class 40 hauled Container working out of Holyhead took place on June 10th 1985 when D200 was provided for 4K59, the 17.05 departure to Basford Hall. Here it is seen storming through Prestatyn. It would also be provided to replace failed 47409 from Bangor on 4H59, the 05.25 to Trafford Park on November 5th that year so ending 15 years on this duty. **Dave Sallery.**

Page 55. April 21st 1984 Mostyn. 40086 heads the Conway Crusader II railtour towards Chester on the return leg. This tour also featured 40118/122/192 along with 50007 that paired up with 40192 for a leg between Llandudno Junction and Blaenau Ffestiniog during the day! **David Rostance.**

Below. 40143 heads into the morning sun at Mostyn with 6E36 the Anglesey Aluminium sidings to Immingham empty Coke covered hoppers. August 9th 1984. **Peter Hanahoe.**

North Wales

North Wales

Above. Greenfield near Flint on October 27th 1981. 40087 heads a 6F27 loaded ballast originating at Penmaenmawr past the Courtaulds works located there at the time. **David Rapson.**

Below. 27th June 1981 and 40057 passes Bagillt with 1A66 the 09.16 Llandudno to Euston via Birmingham New St. Class 40's often worked MK2 air conditioned stock and MK3's on Euston to Llandudno services on summer Saturdays, not pleasant for the passengers! **Peter Hanahoe.**

North Wales

Above. Flint station, May 30th 1980. 40034 "Accra" brings the 11.30 from Bangor to a stand. This was during a period of several years when Class 40's reigned supreme on Manchester Victoria to North Wales services. The end came for this example in January 1984 due to the curse of the bogie fracture! **Arnie Furness.**

Below. September 3rd 1977 and York based 40056 has just passed Shotton Low Level station on 1M59 the 09.33 Scarborough to Llandudno. Apart from a few short periods on loan 40056 was an Eastern region loco for the first 23 years or so of its life before seeing out the final 2 years based at Carlisle Kingmoor prior to withdrawal in September 1984. **David Rapson.**

Above. 40107 approaches Shotton Low Level heading 2D99, the 15.40 Manchester Victoria to Bangor on April 24th 1980. By August that year it would be placed in store at Horwich Works of all places waiting a decision on possible scrapping. However a reprieve was granted with an overhaul of some kind taking place at Crewe Works later that month. The stay of execution did not last long though and by the end of 1981 final withdrawal came at Wigan Springs Branch. This was followed by a move back to Crewe Works, although this time it was a one way trip! Final disposal came in November 1984. **David Rapson.**

North Wales

Above. 40056 at Queensferry at the head of 6F27, the 10.13 Penmaenmawr to St Helens CCE ballast duty on October 28th 1982. It had recently been transferred to Carlisle Kingmoor from Healey Mills having been an Eastern Region loco for the first 20 years of its life.

Below. July 15th 1978, Queensferry again. Springs Branch allocated 40143 shows signs of a recent overhaul as it heads west on 1D41 the 14.30 Crewe to Holyhead. Withdrawn on the final day of regular class 40 operation the end for 40143 came at Crewe Works in October 1986.
Both David Rapson.

North Wales

Above. 40044 is seen at Sandycroft near Shotton working a westbound van train to Bangor on April 24th 1984. This particular loco was involved in a major derailment at Chinley whilst heading a 7Z20 Peak Forest to Whitemoor stone train on September 16th 1978. Repairs were carried out at Crewe Works during an 18 month period and it went on to remain in service right up until the last day of regular Class 40 operation on January 22nd 1985. **Tom Derrington/Martin Loader collection.**

Below. Mold Junction, August 19th 1978. York based 40067 heads for Llandudno on 1M71, the 08.41 Saturdays only departure from York. **David Rostance.**

North Wales

Above. D332 (40132) is seen on the approaches to Chester at Mold Junction heading 1A55, a morning departure from Holyhead to Euston on the 22nd of July 1969 The once extensive yard located here can be seen in the background. Withdrawn in March 1982 it would be one of a few of the class cut up by Vic Berry Leicester, some five years later. **The late Keith Holt.**

Below. July 8th 1978 and 40183 heads west past the impressive signal gantries at Mold Junction on 1M48, the 07.57 Leeds to Llandudno summer Saturday working. A return to Yorkshire would take place with 1E82, the 13.44 Llandudno to York later that day. **David Rostance**

North Wales

Above. The Chester & Connah's Quay Railway ran from Chester Northgate to Shotton and later formed part of a freight only line from Mickle Trafford Junction to Dee Marsh. This remained open until 1992 although it had been singled following a closure between April 1984 and August 1986. In this view 40022 "Laconia" is seen approaching Dee Marsh Junction at Sealand working 8L40, the 13.00 Garston to Dee Marsh coal empties on June 3rd 1980.

Below. Springs Branch allocated 40094 passes through Sealand on 8T56, the 14.09 trip working from Northwich to Dee Marsh. September 25th 1980. **Both David Rapson.**

North Wales

Above. The CFPS's very own 40145 at Dee Marsh East Junction heading 8Z25, the 08.30 Dee Marsh to Tinsley on September 24th 1979. Several Merseyrail class 503 EMU's can be seen in the background waiting onward movement to the scrap yard.

Below. 40108 heads 1L00, the 08.15 Marlyebone to Euston "North West Rambler II" charter towards Dee Marsh East Junction on January 13th 1979. Cold weather resulted in a number of changes in itinerary during the day including the need to start the tour from High Wycombe. 40108 worked the full North West section of the tour. **Both David Rapson.**

North Wales

North Wales

Above. May 18th 1977 and 40020 "Franconia" departs Dee Marsh on the 8T71 trip working to Warrington Arpley.

Page 64. With the feel of the very hot summer of 1976 in the air, 40111 is seen at Sealand on 6L31, a 12.00 departure from Stanlow bound for the nearby Shotwick sidings. Recent repairs to the No1 end of the loco following a fatal collision in Scotland the previous October are evident. July 5th 1976.

Below. July 17th 1979. 40024 "Lucania" at Dee Marsh heading 6F26, an evening working from Shotwick returning empty bogie fuel tanks to Stanlow. **All David Rapson.**

North Wales

Above. Ex works Healey Mills based 40148 departs Dee Marsh on 8Z49 bound for Aber Junction on May 27th 1976. It would be interesting to know how far it worked this service!

Page 67. A very tatty 40136 is seen heading 8J16, the 15.23 to Croes Newydd out of Dee Marsh on August 26th 1976. This was one of the final two Class 40's to remain in green livery prior to repaint into BR blue, the other being 40171. D322, 40039 and 40106 would never receive blue livery.

Below. 40094 reverses a 9X10 exceptional load conveying bridge girders from Ellesmere Port into Dee Marsh yard on September 17th 1980. **All David Rapson.**

North Wales

North Wales

Above. 40125 departs Dee marsh heading 8K64, the 09.03 working to Etruria near Stoke. The date is September 19th 1975 and the surroundings are full of industrial activity. A London Midland loco throughout its life, 40125 was withdrawn relatively early, this coming at the end of May 1981.

Below. Just as a freak snow shower hits the area, 40011 "Mauretania" is seen paired up with 40023 "Lancastria" to work an 8X68 11.30 departure from Dee Marsh to Birkenhead North with brand new EMU's 507017 and 507018 in tow. The train had originated at BREL York Works where these units had been built. Date, March 22nd 1979. **Both David Rapson.**

North Wales

Above. Healey Mills based 40176 passes BSC Shotton steelworks on September 5th 1979 heading for Llanwern on 6Z31, an 08.00 departure conveying steel carrying empties. This was during a period of transition which culminated in the end of steel making on this site and loss of no less than 6,000 jobs in February 1980. Today the site remains open as a state of the art steel coating plant owned by Tata Steel but only employing a few hundred people.

Below. A rather clean 40135 departs Dee Marsh on October 2nd 1979 on 8T56, the 14.09 trip to Northwich. By May 1988 it would become the property of the CFPS! **Both David Rapson.**

North Wales

Above. May 21st 1979 and 40118 is seen crossing Hawarden Bridge on the approach to Dee Marsh at the head of 8F13, the 08.42 departure from Croes Newydd. **David Rapson.**

Below. Rhydymwyn is located on what was the Mold to Denbigh line. Closed to passenger traffic in 1964 the line remained open to serve nearby Hendre quarry for several years before closure. However, it was reopened for a period in the early 1970's as a loading point for pipes used in a pipeline from Rhosgoch on Anglesey to Stanlow, see page 17. In this very rare view of a train in this location during this period, 40183 can be seen at Rhydymwyn with empties for loading and return to Rhosgoch on July 12th 1974. **John Hobbs.**

North Wales

Above. An unidentified Class 40 passes Hope between Wrexham and Shotton heading a Royal Train from Wrexham on May 17th 1976. It then travelled down the Mold branch to layover near to Padeswood before continuing to Oxenholme. This was probably the last passenger train to visit the Mold branch, a line that was open at the time to serve the nearby Synthite works. **John Hobbs.**

Below. 40052 rolls down Aston Hill just north of Hawarden station on 8F75, the 14.20 Bersham Colliery to Shotwick sidings coal working. Date, May 14th 1980. **David Rapson.**

North Wales

Above. Just over the Welsh border on the Chester to Wrexham line, 40122 passes Rossett heading 1T12, "The Conwy Crusader II" tour on April 21st 1984. **David Rapson.**

Below. The same train as above is seen on Gresford bank heading for Wrexham before changing direction. The return working took it to Bidston via Birkenhead docks, Rockferry, Chester and Crewe before handing over to 40118 for the final leg to Coventry.
Tom Derrington/Martin Loader collection.

North Wales

Above. August 8th 1984 and 40118 passes Croes Newydd crossing at Wrexham General with a mixed freight including scrap carrying wagons owned by Standard Railfreight at the time.

Below. A last look at "D200" hauled railtours in the Wrexham area. February 16th 1985 at Croes Newydd, the "Birkenhead Bandit" heads towards Dee Marsh and onwards to Manchester Victoria via Birkenhead, Hooton, Helsby and Warrington before handing over to 45150 and finally to 85004 for the final leg from Birmingham New Street to Euston. **Both Andrew Gallon.**

North Wales

Above. Brymbo steelworks near Wrexham in 1979. 40122 heads a rake of coal empties towards Croes Newydd yard in the days before the loco gained celebrity status. This was closed by its then owners United Engineering Steels in 1990 with the loss of 1,100 jobs. **Paul Robertson collection.**

Below. 40140 backs a train of coal empties running as 7J67, the 12.26 from Shotwick into Bersham colliery south of Wrexham on October 12th 1979. As with many other deep mines at the time, closure came in December 1986. Note the cut-down Peckett no. 1935 "Hornet" still in use but soon to be replaced by Diesel traction in January 1980. **David Rapson.**

Cambrian Coast & Central Wales

Class 40's were never diagrammed for any duties along The Cambrian and Central Wales routes. However, workings on The Cambrian, particularly to Aberystwyth, were relatively common from the early 1970's onwards especially on summer dated day excursions from the North West, Yorkshire and Midlands. These became more commonplace following withdrawal of the majority of the Class 24's from 1977 onwards when it was possible to see several Class 40 hauled passenger trains traverse the route on summer weekends. In addition, a wide range of railtours were Class 40 hauled, sometimes with a class 24 or 25 attached to provide assistance. Other than the occasional ballast duty the class was not used on any freight workings, what few there were!

Appearances on the Central Wales route from Craven Arms through to South Wales were few and far between being restricted to charter trains although 40174 worked the 1541 Shrewsbury to Swansea (DMU drag) as far as Llandridnod Wells April 7th 1977. The most recent visit was by CFPS owned 40145 heading "The Welsh Central Liner II" railtour from Crewe via Derby on March 3rd 2007. This followed in the footsteps of 40035 which had worked "The Welsh Central Liner" exactly 23 years to the day before on March 3rd 1984, see page 81.

The following pages provide some examples of the Class 40 hauled passenger duties seen on both the Cambrian and Central Wales lines up to the present day.

Above. Welshpool station and 40171 is paired up with 24087 on July 6th 1974 whilst heading a Saturday excursion train. 40171 would go on to be one of the last of the class to receive blue livery, not being applied until its final classified repair at Crewe Works in October 1976 by which time its external appearance was appalling! Note, this is the site of the original Welshpool station. When the Welshpool bypass was constructed a new station was built. This was opened in 1993, the original one shown above became a craft centre and remains open in that form. **David Edwards.**

Cambrian Coast

Above. With little more than three months left in traffic, the sole surviving vacuum only braked member of the class 40009 climbs Talerddig bank on July 22nd 1984 with the CFPS operated "Cambrian Coast Express" that ran from Manchester Victoria to Aberystwyth. **Geoff Griffiths.**

Below. What is thought to be the first Class 40 hauled service north of Barmouth ran on April 3rd 1971 behind 215 "Aquitania" which worked a Wirral Railway Circle special to Porthmadog. Here it is seen passing Gogarth halt just west of Dovey Junction on the outbound journey.
E N Kneale/Steve Morris collection.

Cambrian Coast

Above. 40122 is assisted by 25288 as it reaches Talerddig summit working "The Welsh Thunderer" railtour from Stalybridge to Pwllheli on June 7th 1986. The pair then worked the 2J36 Pwllheli to Porthmadog and 1A85 Porthmadog to Euston as far as Shrewsbury before 40122 took the railtour over from 37426/428 for the final leg to Stalybridge single handed. **David Rostance.**

Below. April 7th 1973. 320 (40120) at Tywyn with a "Cambrian Coast Express" charter from Crewe to Aberystwyth via Tywyn for a visit to the Talyllyn railway. **The late Ted Baxendale.**

Cambrian Coast

Above. An early 1970's view of 343 (40143) waiting to return from Aberystwyth with a summer Saturday advertised excursion. **The late Ted Baxendale.**

Below. July 10th 1977. Well of the beaten track, Healey Mills based 40193 is seen at Aberystwyth waiting to depart for York on a return excursion. An early end to the career of this loco came after sustaining collision damage at Lackenby steelworks during October 1981. **Steve Burdett.**

Cambrian Coast

Above. Having worked in from Bradford earlier in the day, York based 40072 waits to return home from Aberystwyth on August 4th 1974 with a train full of Yorkshire day trippers. A transfer to Haymarket would come the following March before being one of four Class 40's withdrawn during 1977 as life expired, the others being 40048/054/059. **Barry Wynne.**

Below. 40106 is seen at Aberystwyth on a charter from Crewe during December 4th 1982. A return trip to Devils Bridge behind steam loco No7 was included in the itinerary. **John Mahon.**

Cambrian Coast

Above. June 26th 1978 and 40025 "Lusitania" shunts the stock of 1L75, an adex from Stalybridge to Barmouth, following arrival at its destination. 40025 worked the train throughout. Three loco hauled services visited Barmouth on this day. **Steve Burdett.**

Below. 40122 and 25288 run around the stock of "The Welsh Thunderer" railtour after arrival at its final destination Pwllheli on June 7th 1986. The Class 25 was added due to a broken windscreen on 40122. See also page 77. **Ron Watson-Jones.**

Central Wales

Above. A rare appearance of a Class 40 on the Central Wales line occurred on March 3rd 1984 when 40035 "Apapa" was provided to work "The Welsh Central Liner" charter which had started from Plymouth. It worked the service from Bristol and back to Severn Tunnel Junction and is seen here during a photo stop at Llanwrtyd Wells. See also page 86. **Andrew Goodson.**

Below. Fast forward exactly 23 years to March 3rd 2007 and here is the CFPS's 40145 posing in the same location with the "The Welsh Central Liner II" tour. This ran out via Derby and Cardiff before returning via Central Wales and back to Crewe, again via Derby. **Steve Morris.**

South & West Wales

Whilst Class 40's were never commonplace in South, and particularly West Wales, they did in fact have several diagrammed freight workings into the region and even within South Wales itself. Sightings on passenger duties were less common and restricted to the odd Crewe-Cardiff service during the late 1970's filling in for the booked Class 25 as well as Sunday diversions and charter trains. The only exception to this was the diagrammed use of 40122 during several months in 1987 on a Holyhead to Cardiff passenger service, mostly from and to Crewe.

Severn Tunnel Junction drivers were the only South Wales men passed out on the class with driver training taking place from 1979 onwards. Traction Inspector Dennis Flood recalls training twenty six STJ drivers in 1981 using a three day Class 37 conversion course. He recounts "I would arrange with Crewe Control to give me a vacuum brake only loco one day and a dual brake locomotive on another for static training purposes. On the third day I would take one out for driver practical handling on whatever train I decided was appropriate. I took one to Oakdale Colliery, on one occasion. The Signalman at Lime Kiln Junction nearly fell out of his box..!!" There is a photo of Dennis with two drivers at Severn Tunnel Junction published in Jane's Railway Year 1982 edition with 40009, 40087 and 40136 in view. The main duties covered were a STJ to Llandeilo Junction service along with one to Exeter Riverside and inter-regional workings to Carlisle and Mossend as far as Warrington which STJ men worked to Hereford. As early as 1978 the class worked to Cardiff on occasions on the 01:40 MWO Ellesmere Port to Hereford which was regularly extended to the Thomas Ness plant at Caerphilly on Wednesdays but with a Class 37 normally taking over at Cardiff. Examples include 40182 on 23rd August, 40186 on 30th August and 40091 right through to Caerphilly on September the 13th! From August 1979 they took over the 01:40 WFO Ellesmere Port to Severn Tunnel Junction and the 09:20 return and from October the 08:00 STJ to Mossend and 18:36SX Garston to STJ workings. The author recalls seeing 40122 at Hereford heading for STJ on an inter-regional working as late as the summer of 1986!

Above. 40044 is seen at Pontypool at the head of 6V39, the 08.40 Mossend to Severn Tunnel Junction which it would have worked from Warrington Walton Old Junction. It is August 13th 1984 and with the end of regular Class 40 operation approaching, sightings of the class on this duty were becoming rarer by the week. **Carl Brunnock.**

South & West Wales

Above. 40024 "Lucania" pauses at Pontypool Road for a photostop whilst working "The South Wales Whistler" back east having visited Swansea and Carmarthen during the day. April 28th 1984. See also pages 94 and the front cover. **Paul Haywood.**

Below. 40057 heads a short ballast train through Cwmbran on a misty May 31st 1984. The previous September it had worked well into West Wales on a railtour, see page 96. **Carl Brunnock.**

South & West Wales

Above. With just over three months left in service, 40099 passes through Cwmbran on July the 12th 1984 working 1Z36, an 18.00 Cardiff to Holyhead charter service.

Below. 40177 at the head of a lightly loaded 6S78, the 18.20 Severn Tunnel Junction to Mossend passes through Cwmbran on April 27th 1984. **Both Carl Brunnock.**

South & West Wales

Above. 40060 has a dead 47448 as part of the consist of 6S78 through Cwmbran on September 14th 1984. This service was often used to move locos to home depots for repair, 47448 heading for Crewe.

Below. Our last look at 6S78 as 40001 powers through Cwmbran with a well loaded train on the 7th of September 1983. **Both Carl Brunnock.**

South & West Wales

Above. Just over the Welsh border, 40035 "Apapa" is paired up with 45064 at the head of "The Welsh Central Liner" tour on March 3rd 1984. The Class 45 had been added at Gloucester to provide steam heat although it was removed at Port Talbot. 37266 was also used for the same purpose during the day. Starting at Plymouth at 04.40, this tour covered the Central Wales line, see page 81, and the line to Sudbrook from Severn Tunnel Junction, during the day.

Below. On August 7th 1983 40029 "Saxonia" was provided to work 1V79, the 08.25 Manchester Piccadilly to Bristol Temple Meads. Diverted via Gloucester and Severn Tunnel Junction due to engineering works it is seen waiting to run around the train at STJ. Later that day it would return north on the 14.25 Bristol to Leeds as far as Derby. **Both Carl Brunnock.**

South & West Wales

Above. Having departed Swansea behind 37229, "The Devon Belle" railtour to Paignton was hauled by 40079 from Newport and back as far as Severn Tunnel Junction. Here it is seen on the outbound working passing STJ depot with a wide range of motive power on display. September 16th 1984.
Carl Brunnock.

Left. Running from Crewe on May 23rd 1987 behind 40122 with tail assistance from 37280 as required, the "Gwent Valley Explorer" is seen at Aberbeeg Junction en route Ebbw Vale during the day.
The tour also visited Machen quarry, Barry Island and Oakdale Colliery as part of the itinerary, see page 88.
Steve Morris.

South & West Wales

Above. The "Gwent Valley Explorer", see previous page, makes its final call of the day at Oakdale Colliery prior to heading back to Crewe via Newport on May 23rd 1987. 40122 made a number of appearances in and out of Cardiff during this period. See pages 92 and 93. **Carl Brunnock.**

Below. Unreliability of the diagrammed pool of Canton allocated class 25's during the mid to late 1970's led to several class 40 substitutions for the out and back workings from Crewe to Cardiff. In this view 40112 has been used to work the 12.25 from Crewe on August 25th 1979, seen leaving Newport. Other examples known to have covered this duty include 40024/026/118/177 and 182. **Steve Burdett.**

South & West Wales

Above. Class 40's were used on 3V20, the 15.10 Manchester to Bristol and return Red Star parcels service a number of times. Here, 40009 is seen on arrival at Newport prior to running around to head for Bristol. The date is October 12th 1984. Within a month 40009 would be withdrawn.

Below. To get it to the area to work a railtour the next day, see page 95, 40057 was used on a Saga special from Workington to Tenby as far as Cardiff on September 10th 1983. In this view it can be seen heading west from Newport. **Both Carl Brunnock.**

South & West Wales

Above. Class 40 sightings west of Newport were rare. In this view 40 160 is seen at Marshfield with a train of LPG tanks, probably heading for Baglan Bay. April 27th 1983. **Martin Davis.**

Below. During the summer of 1980, 1M61 the 10.15 Scarborough to Birmingham was extended to Cardiff on a number of occasions. In this view, a particularly rateable York based 40037 is seen following arrival at Cardiff Central on June 28th 1980 having worked throughout. **Phil Lindsey.**

South & West Wales

Above. 40116 runs light towards Radyr yard on March 24th 1979. What it was doing there is a mystery! **Ron Halestrap.**

Right. A rare shot of a 40 inside the servicing shed at Canton. 40028 is being prepared for the return of the CFPS "Christmas Cracker II" tour on December 17th 1983. **David F Spencer.**

Bottom left. Having come to the aid of 25058, 40177 has just arrived at Cardiff on the 12.25 from Crewe. The date is February 18th 1978 and was during a period when several Class 40's assisted or completely substituted Class 25's on Crewe to Cardiff workings due to reliability issues with the booked traction. **Alan Lea.**

Bottom right. February 26th 1977 and 40028 "Samaria" is stabled in Radyr yard with the stock of a football special that had run from Liverpool in conjunction with an FA Cup game between Cardiff City and Everton. Two more specials were operated that day, all laying over in Radyr yard during the game. Apart from the class 47 hauled one seen in this image, 40120 was also present but out of view. **Dean Tabor.**

South & West Wales

Above. Wigan Springs Branch allocated 40181 is seen stabled on No1 road at the East end of Canton servicing shed on May 9th 1982. How it got there is uncertain but it could have been as a result of repairs that could not be carried out at Severn Tunnel Junction. **Lewis Bevan.**

Below. Each weekday during the week commencing May 25th 1987, 40122 worked the 1V03 05.15 Holyhead to Cardiff and 1M86 13.00 return from and to Crewe. In this image it is seen at Canton carriage shed waiting to depart for Cardiff Central on the 5M86 ECS working to take up the return service to Holyhead as far as Crewe on May 27th 1987. **Steve Morris.**

South & West Wales

Above. On the first day of 40122 covering the Holyhead to Cardiff turn in May 1987, it is seen waiting departure from Cardiff Central with the 13.00 to Holyhead. May 25th 1987. **Mark Simms.**

Below. February 25th 2006. 40145 has just arrived at platform 3 Cardiff Central after working "The Welsh Whistler" railtour from Crewe. The return would result in an unfortunate failure for 40145 on the approach to Stoke Works Junction due to a fractured air pipe. After several hours this resulted in a rescue from 47714 and eventually a tow back to Crewe by 47815 from Birmingham New Street. **Steve Morris.**

South & West Wales

South & West Wales

Above. A diagrammed working for the class, 40183 is seen at Port Talbot working 6C59 the 14.00 Llandeilo Junction to Severn Tunnel Junction on June 2nd 1982. **Colin Baker.**

Page 94. 40024 "Lucania" climbs Stormy Bank near Margam working "The South Wales Whistler" railtour towards Swansea on April 28th 1984. **Phil Lindsey.**

Below. Probably the only "non railtour" hauled Class 40 passenger working into Swansea took place on January 21st 1979 when 40010 "Empress of Britain" was provided for an 09.35 Edinburgh to Swansea "Rugex" from Crewe. Here it presents a somewhat unusual sight on the blocks at Swansea High Street having just arrived at its destination. **Alan Lea.**

South & West Wales

Above. Thursday May 12th 1983 and 40158 heads a ballast working at Briton Ferry. This was a particularly unusual duty for a Class 40, especially as it was outside the normal weekend track maintenance period. **Richard Molyneux.**

Above right. Probably the furthest into West Wales that a Class 40 travelled was on September 11th 1983 when 40057 worked the "Pembroke Haven Harbourer" railtour from Severn Tunnel Junction to Pembroke Dock and Fishguard Harbour. In this view it can be seen running around the stock at Carmarthen to take up the leg to Pembroke Dock. **John Stephens.**

Below. Later in the day, the above service waits to depart Fishguard Harbour on the return to Severn Tunnel Junction where it would hand over to 37266 or 37127, depending on what portion of the train you were travelling in! Portion 1 behind 37266 ended up at Bristol Temple Meads via Birmingham whilst portion 2 behind 37127 terminated at Plymouth with 46025 taking over at Bristol for the final part of the tour, a fine day out indeed! **Steve Hale.**